THINKING ABOUT CRIME PREVENTION

PERFORMANCE INDICATORS

Nick Tilley

POLICE RESEARCH GROUP
CRIME DETECTION AND PREVENTION SERIES: PAPER NO 57
LONDON: HOME OFFICE POLICE DEPARTMENT

Editor: Gloria Laycock
Home Office Police Research Group
50 Queen Anne's Gate
London SW1H 9AT

Crime Prevention Unit Papers

The Home Office Police Research Group (PRG) was formed in 1992 to carry out and manage research relevant to the work of the police service and Home Office Policy Divisions. One of the major Police Departments divisions which acts as customer for the PRG is the Home Office Crime Prevention Unit which was formed in 1983 to promote preventive action against crime. It has a particular responsibility to disseminate information on crime prevention topics.

The object of the present series of occasional papers is to present research material in a way which should help and inform practitioners, whose work can help reduce crime.

ISBN 1-85893-320-X

Foreword

In December 1993, the Home Secretary wrote to Chief Constables setting out his proposals for key objectives for policing in 1994/95. He noted, in doing so, that no high level performance indicator was currently available in relation to the prevention of crime, although the Home Secretary had attached great importance to police work in this area. Further work to develop the ideas associated with performance measurement in relation to crime prevention was promised.

This report represents one aspect of that further work. The report is not intended to direct forces in this area but rather, as its title implies, to provide some thoughts on how progress can be made. The report represents the views of a number of serving police officers as well as the relevant research literature. If the proposals are seen as helpful by police forces then there will be quite a bit of preparatory work in bringing them to fruition. Nevertheless, if crime prevention is to be given the priority it deserves, then performance against it must in some way be measured. This report represents a first and significant step in that direction.

I M BURNS
Deputy Under Secretary of State
Home Office
November 1994

Acknowledgements

I am indebted to a large number of people for their help in preparing this paper. I have had invaluable formal and informal discussions with many police officers. These include those serving in the Devon and Cornwall, Cleveland, Greater Manchester, Leicestershire, Metropolitan Police, Nottinghamshire, and Thames Valley forces, as well as officers involved in training at the Crime Prevention Centre at Stafford, some working for Her Majesty's Inspectorate, and some within the Home Office Police Research Group. I have also talked about indicators with a number of university academics, including both criminologists and methodologists. I have consulted those within the Audit Commission concerned with police performance. Finally, Home Office Researchers and Officials have been generous with their advice. There was full agreement on one thing only: that there was no existing satisfactory high level crime prevention performance indicator and that devising a plausible one was a pig of a problem! Successive drafts of the paper have again been patiently read and helpfully commented on by police, academics and Home Office personnel. Whilst I have to accept responsibility for what is presented here, any merit in the arguments reflects efforts to canvass and take advantage of a very wide a range competent opinion.

Nick Tilley
August 1994

The Author

Nick Tilley is a reader at The Nottingham Trent University. He is attached part-time to the Home Office Police Research Group.

Contents

List of Tables

List of Figures

1. Introduction

There are two immediate origins to this paper. First, in June 1993 the White Paper on Police Reform (Cm 2281) mooted 'work with the local community in crime prevention' as one possible initial Government key objective for policing. It was also stated that a small number of Key Performance Indicators (KPIs) would support the key objectives. Following this, on December 3rd 1993, the Home Secretary wrote to Chief Constables announcing key objectives for 1994-5, amongst which the third is **'to target and prevent crimes which are a particular local problem in partnership with the public and other local agencies'**. He goes on to say that **'progress towards these objectives will be measured by key performance indicators set out in the Appendix'**. The Appendix states in regard to the crime prevention performance indicator: **'No high level indicator is currently available. Work on developing such an indicator for 1995/96 will be taken forward over the next year, aimed at measuring the effectiveness of crime prevention initiatives'**. Second, the Metropolitan Police have asked for advice about possible performance indicators to assess the work of Crime Prevention Officers.

The following discussion does not dwell on whether performance indicators are desirable or undesirable *per se*. Instead, it takes the use of PIs as a given, and considers ways forward both in relation to the Home Secretary's national objective for crime prevention and, going slightly beyond the immediate interests of the Metropolitan Police, in relation to the assessment of crime prevention effectiveness within individual forces.

In thinking about what PIs to use, it is important to be clear about what they can and cannot do, and to be sensitive to their potentially undesirable unintended consequences. This is dealt with, albeit very briefly, in Section 2. Section 3 turns to the particular difficulties which have been met in efforts to devise high level performance indicators for crime prevention, and highlights shortcomings in most of the current contenders. Section 4 discusses in some detail repeat victimisation as a KPI, since this, whilst not without problems, appears currently to be the most plausible candidate, even though it will probably need some supplementation along lines to be indicated. Section 5 considers some objections to the use of repeat victimisation as a KPI. Section 6 presents some possibilities for PIs for use within individual forces in assessing their crime prevention work, at the same time fitting this with efforts to attain the national objective. Section 7 summarises the main conclusions to be drawn from the preceding discussion.

The discussion of high level national KPIs pays little explicit attention to partnership as such, but rather emphasises the outcome effectiveness of crime prevention efforts, on the grounds that partnership can be deemed to have played a key part in the local determination of crimes to target. It is also the case, of course, that most crime prevention measures cannot be implemented without the cooperation of the public and/or other agencies. Since partnership is a *sine qua non* of effective locally targeted crime prevention work it does not require separate measurement within a high level indicator focusing on outcomes. When we turn to PIs for individual forces, however, it will become important, among other things, to find where partnerships are operating and assess how successful they are being in attaining crime prevention outcome aims. Good practice in this area can then be disseminated in the usual ways.

The discussion which follows is based on examination of background literature relating to crime prevention and PIs as well as discussions with police officers in seven forces, Home Office officials, HMIC officers, staff at HOCPC, and those working at the Audit Commission on police performance. Their advice is gratefully acknowledged.

2. Performance Indicators for Performance Indicators

What PIs can and cannot do

Performance indicators do not directly measure quality of performance. The term 'Performance Indicator' needs to be taken seriously. An indicator is a pointer. It is not a direct measure. It suggests a line of further examination. Baldness may be used as a rough indicator of maleness or of increasing age or possibly even of virility! It is a direct measure of none of these, and plenty of exceptions could be found. Equally, profitability may be used as an indicator of efficiency in the management of a commercial enterprise, but again plenty of exceptions could be found. Indicators are better or worse according to how precisely they tap the underlying feature they are supposed to assess. What they suggest will, however, always need to be interpreted with care.

Performance indicators do not and cannot be used to evaluate the outcome-effectiveness of individual pieces of work. What produces the precise outcome effects of any particular initiative will often be highly complex and will require very detailed analysis. To assess the degree to which something has worked will necessitate, for example, careful articulation of the ways in which the measures introduced are supposed to have their effects; a specification of the conditions needed for these effects to be brought about in the ways they are supposed to work; particulars of diverse aspects of the 'before' situation; efforts to disentangle effects of extraneous events and so on (see Ekblom 1990; Ekbom & Pease, Forthcoming; Pawson & Tilley 1994). Performance indicators at best give only gross estimates of possible overall impact. The further the PI from the particulars of any initiative, the rougher the significance of the measure.

If published, high level Performance Indicators may provide citizens, who through their taxes pay for public services, with a set of suggestive questions about whether they are or are not being served effectively, efficiently and equitably by public sector organisations. PIs can constitute, thus, one vehicle for accountability to the public.

High level Performance Indicators can provide government with one way of ascertaining whether public services, for which elected representatives have ultimate responsibility on behalf of the community, seem to be attending effectively to the priorities set for them[1]. Where public sector organisations are given operational independence, for whatever reason, objective setting and performance measurement provide a residual route to exercising some control (Smith forthcoming). PIs can thus provide a way in which service providers can be made accountable to government.

---

1   See Annex A for a discussion of currently preferred ways of organising police crime prevention work.

Within public sector organisations PIs can be used by management as a check on how well individual elements are functioning, and suggest areas where change may be called for. There can be a feedback loop from objective setting to performance measurement through PIs to organisational change.

PIs can be used to motivate improvements in performance by sensitising those responsible for service delivery to apparent levels of effectiveness and to changes in them. PIs can reinforce success and thereby encourage good practice. They can also point to areas where further attention may be needed.

To whatever use PIs are put, they will, as is acknowledged in the Police Reform White Paper (para 7.11), need to be rounded out. *PIs never fully speak for themselves.*

PI dangers

The previous passage suggests that PIs may be a used as a handy management tool, and that they may also provide a vehicle for public and political accountability for the effective, economical and equitable provision of public services. Unfortunately, PIs can also harbour dangers. Smith (forthcoming) identifies eight:

   a) 'Tunnel vision', or emphasis on only the quantifiable, neglecting unquantifiable aspects of performance.

   b) 'Suboptimisation', or the production of lower quality of service overall by concentrating on narrowly defined (measured) activity at the expense of attending to wider overall objectives.

   c) 'Myopia', or failure to attend to legitimate longer term objectives.

   d) 'Measure fixation', or concentration on what is being measured rather than the service the measurement is intended to signify.

   e) 'Misrepresentation', or deliberate corruption of data.

   f) 'Misinterpretation', or uncritical acceptance of the face value meaning of results.

   g) 'Gaming', or strategic management of behaviour, including periodic deliberate underperformance, to produce easy targets and apparent success when advantageous.

   h) 'Ossification', or inflexible pursuit of defined performance objectives set at one particular time.

To Smith's eight at least two more might be added:

i) 'Demoralisation', or loss of confidence and commitment amongst workers delivering services deemed not to count or to be counted inappropriately.

j) 'Discreditability', or public scepticism - brought about through sabotage of enforced PIs by disillusioned workers.

PI benchmarks

Performance needs to be assessed against some kind of standard. Very commonly no standard can be identified other than the performance of other equivalent organisations or units of organisations. Thus the creation of league tables is often deemed to be a necessary corollary of PI development in order to make sense of the results for any individual unit. League tables can also potentially mislead, since the circumstances facing one group pursuing their objective will differ from that facing another. Efforts to explore a 'value-added' PI for schools rather than one based on a crude examination results represents an attempt to recognise that not all schools begin with the same raw material with their intakes.

PIs and their benchmarks need also to relate as closely as possible to intended outcomes rather than outputs. Outcomes refer to the results of what is done whilst output refers to the volume of activity. Concentrating on outcomes avoids preoccupation with a particular means rather than concentrating on the ends being pursued for the public. Where there is scope for debate, difference and uncertainty about how ends may best be achieved, and where means available differ from one area to another it will be especially important to focus performance measurement on outcome objectives.

Quantitative benchmarks and subsequent performance scores are useful to enable clear year on year comparisons to be made. Where league tables are to be created there need to be common, unambiguous methods of measurement and calculation.

If some point outside the performance of other nominally equivalent units can be found as a basis for measuring performance, this may avoid the need for league tables which are easily misinterpreted. Maximising the sensitivity of performance scores to particulars of local conditions is in any case desirable, given difference in initial circumstances.

The ideal: PI in the sky?

The following desiderata for police crime prevention PIs, most of which follow from the earlier discussion in this section, enjoyed wide support amongst those consulted during the course of this work.

a) The PIs should relate as directly and as accurately as possible to priority intended outcomes of crime prevention work.

b) Efforts to attain success as measured through the PIs should not divert police efforts from the main task of crime prevention. More positively, the performance indicators selected should help focus attention on effective crime prevention work.

c) Efforts to attain success as measured through PIs should not lead the police to compromise other ends they may wish to pursue.

d) The indicators should be quantitative, and ratio measurements are to be preferred.

e) The indicators should be easily understandable.

f) The data used for the indicators should be collectable at minimal cost, or if not already available the work in their assembly should also yield some benefit to policing practices to offset costs incurred.

g) The PIs should relate specifically to police contributions to crime prevention.

h) The measurement should be credible to the police and the public.

i) The calculation of the PI should be unambiguous.

Clearly few if any high level PIs in any field meet all the types of condition referred to in the above list. The characteristics listed do, though, represent an ideal standard against which possible contenders can be assessed. There will have to be compromises when it comes to crime prevention where, as we shall see, there are particular problems.

3. Difficulties in developing national crime prevention KPIs

The current absence of any satisfactory high level PI for police crime prevention is now widely recognised, as are the problems of devising one. The problems in devising indicators have been noted periodically for at least the last decade (see Morris & Heal 1981). These include difficulties in measuring absence of events; wide pseudo-random fluctuations in local crime rates, where separating out the effect of crime prevention efforts requires detailed analysis, and the collection of a wide range of data; national changes, notably in policy, in the economy and in the availability and design of goods, which impact on crime in ways beyond local control; the inability of (expensive) crime surveys to pick out local patterns of change, except when tailored to very small areas; the variability in public reporting and police recording practices which undermine somewhat the usefulness of police data; and, as already indicated, the fact that some local practices, especially those associated with interagency interventions, are beyond the direct control of the police.

Against these general problems let us consider briefly the currently used crime prevention PI and some other possible contenders:

a) Number of Neighbourhood Watches

Home Office Circular 17/1993 notes the use of '**the number of Neighbourhood Watch schemes per 1000 households**' as a measure of community participation in crime prevention, though it is recognised that this is 'not a direct indicator of police performance.' 'Number of Neighbourhood Watch schemes...' fails on several fronts. What counts as an operating Neighbourhood Watch scheme is far from certain, thus the measure is ambiguous. Neighbourhood Watch schemes are most easily seeded where least needed in crime problem terms (Husain 1988, Mayhew et al 1989) and hence will not measure activity where it is most appropriate. If a function of PIs is to motivate police patterns of behaviour, there is a danger that this one may lead resources to be devoted to the creation of ever more, ever smaller Neighbourhood Watches where crime rates are least serious, at the expense of meeting the needs of high crime areas. There is much more to crime prevention than Neighbourhood Watch and the effectiveness of Neighbourhood Watch is uncertain. Hence, it might not be sensible to use a high level indicator which risks provoking greater attention to Neighbourhood Watch. No-one spoken to during this study considered number of Neighbourhood Watches per 1000 households to be a satisfactory PI, and several believed its effects to be counterproductive.

b) Incidence rates

As an alternative to number of Neighbourhood Watch schemes per 1000 households, the most obvious PI would be the crime incidence rate (crimes per 1000 potential victims). It is generally accepted, however, that alterations in overall national and local rates follow from a host of partially understood and much debated causes beyond the control of local partnerships or the police. Furthermore, measurement of incidence rates raises serious problems. Three particular difficulties surface if recorded crime rates are use. First, rates of reporting crime have changed over time and are generally increasing (Mayhew et al 1992). Hence overall recorded crime rates, which depend on public reporting practices, may not accurately reflect changes in the volume of crime occurring. Second, crime recording practices are variable (Farrington & Dowds 1985), and may be subject, in some cases, to discretion which is used to meet perceived police interests. Third, for some crime categories police and public interest lies in increasing the rate at which incidents are reported, for example racial attacks and domestic violence, and these may lead to apparent, though explicable, increases in incidence rates. Crime surveys raise other problems. They only deal with a sub-set of crimes, which are experienced directly by individuals and households and are typically weak even for some of them, for example domestic violence. They would also be very expensive if undertaken properly by all forces. In addition, it would probably be impractical to use a large enough sample to be able to make meaningful intra-force comparisons.

c) Security surveys

The Audit Commission Report, *Helping with Enquiries: Tackling Crime Effectively*, notes a number of possible crime prevention PIs. It refers to '***number of crime prevention surveys***', '***% of crime prevention surveys acted upon***', and '***repeat victimisation rate***' (Audit Commission 1993). The widely recognised problem with 'number of crime prevention surveys' is that it would take crime prevention backwards, away from that strategic role in dealing with crime which is now widely perceived to be the way forward. Per cent of crime surveys acted upon raises some separate problems. One is that of determining what it means to act on a crime survey. Would any action following a survey count? Would full implementation of recommendations be necessary? Previous research suggests that recommendations are rarely followed fully (Laycock 1989), and it is hard to envisage a simple PI in which a clearly defined cut-off between action and inaction could unambiguously be drawn. There is, moreover, a danger that surveys would be delivered and tailored to score high on the PI (for example by making suggestions that are easy to act on even if ineffective, and/or by only suggesting very minimal work, and/or by offering surveys only to those likely to carry out recommendations in full, perhaps because they are can afford to do so). Security surveys (like Neighbourhood Watch) are means to an end not ends in themselves. The objective is the prevention or reduction or redistribution of crime. It would be preferable to have a PI which came closer to outcome effectiveness. The Audit Commission's third possible crime prevention PI, 'Repeat victimisation rate', is discussed separately in sections 4 and 5, below.

d) Cost-benefit calculations

It was suggested by some spoken to in the course of this work that a **cost-benefit approach** be adopted. This could involve estimating the crime prevention effort output relative to the crime prevention input. This is an attractive suggestion, since it would lead the police to allocate efforts systematically. There are, however, difficulties in measuring output. Not all crime prevention is costly and some effective crime prevention may be very low cost. It would be difficult to find an appropriate unit of output which did not distort the crime prevention efforts made. There might be a temptation to direct advice to the relatively less vulnerable rich businesses and individuals at the expense of their relatively more vulnerable and poorer counterparts simply because the better off could be expected to spend more on security improvements. Such a PI would limit crime prevention to what others can do, and divert attention from what the police can themselves achieve directly. It is a measure of *output* rather than *outcome*, that is the efficacy of the police crime prevention effort.

A second approach to cost-benefit analysis, which was also advocated, would involve estimating the overall costs of crime. This has been undertaken, for example, in Nottingham. Such audits could be carried out periodically and compared year by year to see whether costs have fallen in accordance with crime prevention work. Crime audits are, however, expensive and complex. It would be difficult to light on an agreed way of undertaking them. Moreover, many matters beyond the control of the police affect the costs of crime to an area, and changes in them.

e) Surveys

Surveys are frequently mentioned as a way of collecting data for a performance indicator - they obviously do not themselves constitute PIs. Surveys could cover victims or the general public. They could tap a number of issues in addition to patterns of victimisation, for example crime prevention behaviour, membership of partnerships, knowledge of partnerships, satisfaction with police response, satisfaction with police advice, contact with the police, levels of fear of crime, the impact of crime on respondents' lives, the crime concerns of residents etc. Indeed, the police now survey victims of burglary and of violence, as well as members of the general public, in connection with satisfaction measures already used as PIs.

For the national objective at issue here, however, it is unlikely that any one survey question could yield a single PI or that a combination of questions could unambiguously be scaled to produce a useful general survey-based PI. In addition, to obtain a satisfactory response rate and minimise self selection, interviews would be needed of a randomly selected group. Moreover, a large sample would be needed for meaningful or usable intra-force patterns to be identified. Meeting these requirements would be very costly. In very few forces would the existing sample sizes be adequate to collect data of the volume and quality needed. Even then, major local events may distort responses to some possible questions. Moreover, not all crime prevention relates to individual victims. For example it may be directed to high volume crimes against schools, hospitals or businesses, and existing surveys undertaken by the police to collect data for other PIs would not be able to capture this.

Thus, whilst surveys may yield data which forces may find it useful to collect to measure aspects of their performance, they are not an ideal route to a high level PI for the crime prevention national objective. In the next section, we turn to what is considered a more promising way forward.

Though the crime prevention PI contenders discussed above may be inappropriate for national purposes for the reasons given, we shall return to them when we come to force PIs, where several of the methods may have a part to play in assisting the organisation and management of crime prevention work.

Given the difficulties in devising satisfactory high level crime prevention PIs, and the failure over a longish period to come up with anything satisfactory, one conclusion might be that this is one area of police work which is simply not susceptible to the straightforward performance measurement which is called for. This would be regrettable. Many welcome a key objective concentrating on crime prevention and see advantages in the prospect of a KPI to give it weight. A consequence of permanently assigning the development of a PI into the too tricky tray might well be to decrease police attention to crime prevention as it is perceived not to 'count' in the assessment of performance.

We turn now to repeat victimisation, which has been mooted as a possible source for a PI, to consider first how plausible it would be, second how it would need to be supplemented, and third how it might be implemented in practice as a KPI.

4. Repeat victimisation as a KPI

Farrell & Buckley (1993) have recently mooted the possibility of using repeat victimisation for a performance indicator for particular police crime prevention initiatives. There are several reasons for considering in some detail whether it could also form the basis of a high level national KPI, and if so how it should be formulated and what steps would be needed to implement it.

a) There is a growing literature identifying the greater risk of victimisation faced by those who have already been victimised (Farrell & Pease 1993).

b) The police have already been encouraged in various ways to attend to repeat victimisation (see Annex A).

c) A focus on repeats would encourage concentration of crime prevention efforts on high crime areas since it is here that repeats are found to occur at their highest rate (Trickett et al 1992).

d) Rates of recorded repeat victimisation should, in principle, be calculable from data already routinely collected and held by the police, though as we shall see they are not now easy to extract or analyse.

e) Whilst reporting and recording practices overall are variable across forces and across time, it is less likely that reporting and recording practices for repeats will be variable in quite the same way. That said, it must be acknowledged that good, sympathetic practice, for example in relation to domestic violence and racial attack, may increase the confidence with which victims can call on the police, and hence could impact on rates of reported and recorded repeats.

Before discussing some of the practical difficulties in identifying repeat victimisation from police records, issues of measurement and offence choice need to be considered.

Measurement problems

As already said, it is accepted that matters beyond the control of the police (and local partnerships) are crucial in determining changes in overall crime rates. Yet overall rates of crime affect numbers of expected repeats. They also influence the proportions of incidents which are repeats.

Intuitively, it can be appreciated that with an increase in the overall number of incidents in a given population, if victimisation is distributed randomly the expected number per victim will increase. With any number of incidents greater than one, if the already victimised is open to revictimisation the expected rate of revictimisation will exceed zero, since there is already a (random) chance that they will be picked on again. With increasing numbers of incidents the chances of random reselections increase.

Table 1 (building on a method used by Trickett et al 1992, explained in Annex B) assumes a population of 1,000 potential victims and indicates, for incidence rates of 50, 100, 250, 500, 1,000 and 2,000, the statistically expected prevalence rate (number in population victimised), total number of repeats, and numbers of first, second, third, fourth, and fifth repeats. It also shows the variations in 'expected' rates of *concentration* (average victimisations per victim) as the incidence rate increases.

Table 1: Statistically expected patterns of repeat victimisation at varying incidence rates.										
Incidents/ 1000	Expected prevalence	Expected incidence/ prevalence	Expected number of repeats	Repeats as % of incidents	Expected single incident	Expected one repeat	Expected two repeats	Expected three repeats	Expected four repeats	Expected five repeats
50	49	1.02	1	2%	48	1				
100	95	1.05	5	5%	90	5				
250	221	1.13	29	12%	194	25	2			
500	394	1.27	106	21%	301	81	11	1		
1000	632	1.58	368	37%	353	203	64	11	1	
2000	865	2.31	1135	57%	233	285	215	110	20	2

It can be seen that as the incidence rate rises from 50 to 2000 per 1000 potential victims, the statistically expected proportion of repeat victims to all victims increases from 2% to 57%. Thus, increases in incidence can impact heavily on expected proportions of repeats. Average victimisations per victim is also sensitive to variations in crime incidence. Table 1 shows that the average expected victimisations per victim is 1.02 where there are 50 incidents per 1000 potential victims, but rises to 2.31 where there are 2000 incidents per 1000 potential victims. Variation is thus to be expected from differences in incidence rates. Any significant deviation from expected patterns of victimisation will require special explanation. In practice, any observed pattern is likely to result in quite complex ways from offender choice of victim and from efforts often made by victims following an incident to reduce their risks.

Crime prevention 'success' in repeat victimisation terms would be indicated where a statistically significant alteration is made in the ratio of expected to observed levels of concentration (or, which amounts to much the same thing, in the ratio of expected to observed prevalence rates). These measures, though, would not be immediately meaningful to members of the public. If it is expected that forces will be ranked according to their success as measured by performance indicators[2], it might

---

2   If later suggestions are accepted there will be reduced scope for ranking.

be worth bearing this cost since such a calculation would yield a 'fairer' measure than simple rates of concentration or numbers of repeats which are subject to expected alteration in accordance with variations in incidence rates. And these, it is acknowledged, are beyond plausible control by the police. The advantage of using crude concentration rates is that they are immediately understandable. Also, attention to them should direct efforts to effect overall reductions in high crime areas, which will then impact on rates of revictimisation.[3]

Crimes to include in a repeat victimisation PI

It is necessary to consider which crimes to include in a repeat victimisation PI, and this in turn raises questions about definitions of victim categories. There are various alternative crimes which might be included. The possibilities range from all offences to one in particular. There would be some advantages in taking one or more offences which already have high reporting and recording rates, since changes in reporting and recording practices could otherwise distort figures. This would point us, for example, towards domestic burglary with loss or theft of motor vehicles. This, though, would capture only a small part of the range of offences on which police crime prevention efforts, singly or in partnership, could have an impact. The difficulty with taking all offences is that the definition of the victim will vary, making a single index impossible. For example, street robbery is an offence against an individual, whereas domestic burglary affects households and non-domestic burglary affects schools, businesses etc. A compromise position might be to take a sub-set of offences which are experienced by households and non-domestic addresses - burglary, damage and theft - and aggregate them. These account for a large proportion of crime which is found damaging and distressing. Such a selection would, though, omit all personal crimes and all car crimes, respectively serious and widespread crime categories. In view of the Home Secretary's reference to 'crimes which are a particular local problem', it would seem inappropriate to specify which should be included in the KPI. Rather, in drawing up local policing plans Police Authorities might be asked for each division to specify in advance which crime or crimes are to be special targets for prevention in the forthcoming year, and the repeat victimisation PI could then be used to measure effectiveness.

Aggregating results and creating league tables

The repeat victimisation performance indicator mooted here would enable success to be measured against a statistically expected rate and against previous years

---

3   Higher crime rates are associated with greater gaps between statistically expected and actual concentration of victimisation (Trickett et al 1992). Crime prevention directed at revictimisation will thus lead to a focus on relatively high crime areas.

performance, in ways which do not require league tables for interpretations to be made. That is, a benchmark other than others' performances is available.

If, however, league tables were to be required indexing performance with a common base year would be possible. This could be set, say, at 100. Year on year performance could then be inspected by looking at the change in the index. Indexes for differing divisions could be averaged for any given force and an overall score derived. This would have the advantage that forces would be further motivated to focus on high crime areas, since it is here that there is greatest scope for falls, and hence for attaining a 'good' score.

Problems in identifying repeat victims

Though patterns of repeats can be ascertained from crime surveys and victim surveys, these are difficult, expensive, in some ways unreliable and have partial coverage. They would also, as already suggested, neglect offences against some victim categories, for example schools and businesses.

The alternative to collecting data from victims is to use police records which should, in principle, allow patterns of repeat victimisation to be identified. This has a number of advantages.

a) The police are clearly much better placed to help reduce the risks to known victims than to those where offences have not been reported, and it would be more reasonable to base a KPI on their success here than in preventing revictimisation following offences of which they have no knowledge.

b) It should be much cheaper to reanalyse data being routinely collected than to collect data especially.

c) Coverage would be comprehensive for the offence categories included.

d) The comprehensive coverage would allow some detailed intra-force comparisons which should be helpful for management purposes.

At present, unfortunately police crime records rarely if ever allow patterns of repeats readily to be identified and analysed. The difficulty arises from a failure to include unique victim identifiers (UVIs). Records are kept in a form which allow incidents to be uniquely identified (through the crime number), and for counts to be made of those falling into various Home Office crime categories. Within the very short term repeats may be identifiable through memory, map-pinning or eye-balling lists. It is otherwise difficult to measure rates of repeats, howsoever victims are characterised. It is sometimes possible to take a particular victim and to interrogate a data-base to see whether the name or address appears earlier, though this will not produce reliable results, as we shall see. In any case this procedure would not, of course, allow patterns of repeats across sets of crimes in any area to be identified.

The extent of the problem is revealed starkly from work currently being undertaken in the centre of a Midlands town. There were 330 incidents. The apparent prevalence over one full year, as would be identified by a computer looking for the number of different names and addresses comes to 299, with a corresponding concentration rate of 1.1. The actual prevalence was 216, with a concentration rate of 1.53. Table 2 compares the results of the 'true' and apparent pattern of repeats in more detail.

The differences are explained by variations in ways of identifying the victim. The errors are all one way. Repeated victimisations are always lost, never inadvertently gained. Without UVIs, even with the appropriate software, widespread analyses of patterns of repeats of recorded crime are impossible. Presently it is necessary painstakingly to go through lists of incidents to determine whether victimisations have been repeated.

A single incident could have more than one UVI, depending on analytic purposes. For example a car crime could have the registration number of the vehicle, the driving licence number of the driver or owner or user of the vehicle, the address where the owner/driver/user resides or stays and the site where the incident occurred. Patterns for repeats of any of these might be required. In the case of addresses, a convenient UVI may be the post-code plus number or name[4].

No use could sensibly be made of repeats for a KPI with the present record keeping practices within the police. A capacity systematically to interrogate records for patterns of repeats both overall in a force and in small areas would be invaluable for planning crime prevention as well, perhaps, as other police operations.

If it were to be decided that repeat victimisation should form the basis for a crime prevention KPI, an interim step would have to include the development of revised recording methods and analytic tools. It might be that different forces would approach the task in differing ways, according to their current systems and the scope they offer for modification. Some forces might decide to co-operate in forging a shared system. Refining recording practices along the lines suggested is a larger task

---

4   The Post-code Address File is available on CD-ROM, is updated several times a year, and includes all postal points in the country. Both software and hardware would be needed to develop a data-entry system interfacing streets, post-codes, numbers and names to ensure that address-based UVIs were entered. This is unlikely to remove all errors, but could be designed to ensure that no data would be accepted where address and post code did not match with that on the post-code address file. Further software would be needed to allow prevalence rates, counts of incidents, and patterns of repeats to be read off for varying geographical areas including those covering whole forces.

Table 2: A comparison of the rates of repeat non-domestic burglary as corrected and as apparent from exact recorded same addresses.		
Times burgled	Apparent number of addresses	Corrected number of addresses
1	274	143
2	20	48
3	4	13
4	1	8
5	0	4
Total	299	216

than it might first appear, and some despair of its practicability. Yet having the wherewithal accurately to analyse patterns of crime by person and place is a precondition for informed crime prevention work. It is sobering to find that most non police personnel spoken to have been surprised by the fact that it is not now normally possible.

The method of data entry for recorded crimes could also be used in developing UVIs for reported incidents, whose analysis is important for some purposes, notably domestic violence.

Whilst computerised recording systems are adapted, a short term method of identifying individual victims and measuring rates of repeat victimisation could be by victim interviews, though this would be expensive and, unless conducted by independent professionals, risks yielding fairly low-grade information. Moreover, it would still be necessary to find prevalence rates, which cannot be estimated accurately with most current recording practices.

Prevalence rates: an essential PI bonus

One problem with using repeat victimisation as a sole outcome effectiveness crime prevention KPI is that it fails to acknowledge that considerable effort made by the police, often in partnership with those in other agencies, to act pre-emptively to design out crime risks. There is also the possibility that by reducing risks of repeat victimisation, more victims will be drawn in, that is that prevalence will increase. This may be an acceptable outcome - spreading the misery - but should, perhaps, be recognised in a second, though subsidiary PI.

Another difficulty with a sole focus on repeat victimisation for a PI is that repeats appear to occur both most commonly in high crime areas, which would be expected statistically, but also to exceed by the largest factor the expected rate. In fact in low crime areas whilst rates of revictimisation consistently exceed what would be expected statistically, they do so by only modest amounts (Trickett et al 1992). Moreover, comparing the 1982, 1984 and 1988 British Crime Surveys, whilst increases in the highest crime areas could be explained more by increases in concentration than in prevalence, this was not the case in lower crime areas. Here, more of the increase is explicable by increases in prevalence. In low crime areas, whilst attention to risks of repeats clearly still makes sense, it generally seems to form a much stronger general strategy in higher crime areas. That said, for certain crime categories, for example domestic violence and racial attacks, even in generally low crime areas a focus on repeat victimisation is likely logically to form a core part of any strategy.

It might, thus, be useful to measure prevalence as a secondary PI in order to capture pre-emptive crime prevention, to attend to more fruitful work in low crime areas, and to acknowledge that displacement may occur as a result of efforts to reduce repeats. Moreover, since in order to measure levels of concentration, the repeat victimisation PI, it is necessary to make a measure of prevalence it comes, as it were, free.

It should also be realised that with concentration rates and prevalence rates incidence rates can also be calculated. These, though weak as a source of a KPI for reasons already given, are likely to remain of public interest.

5. A repeat victimisation KPI: some objections

There are many advantages in directing efforts at reducing repeat victimisation, and for this to be a major ingredient in police crime prevention work (see Farrell & Pease 1992, National Board 1994). Measurement of changes in patterns of repeats is probably the best we can now hope for as a solution to the notoriously thorny problem of a crime prevention KPI, and the above discussion has been concerned to help clarify in some detail how this could best be done. It is, however, no panacea. Let us turn to some potential problems which have been raised.

First, as already indicated recorded crime statistics are notoriously problematic. There are two ways in which particular difficulties may arise in relation to repeats and their use as a PI. Both may operate unconsciously. First, police discretion may be used either in decisions to record incidents or to categorise them in ways which present performance in the best light. This may mean that in a 'before' year, maximum numbers of repeats of target incidents may be recorded. Then in the score year these events will be minimised. A solution may be to maintain a target for at least two years, and not to announce changes in advance. Second, police reactions to events may affect victims' dispositions to report repeats. An unsympathetic response may, thus, reduce repeats. For some crime categories such a domestic and racial harassment, prime targets for repeat victimisation prevention strategies, this may be a particular problem. It may be prudent here separately to assess, through independent sample interviews, the victim's views of the service they received from the police, though this will obviously incur costs.

Second, there is more to police crime prevention work that attempting to reduce repeats, and this other, often longer term work, may be in danger of being undervalued and overlooked. In regard to this, it should be remembered that, though key objectives are not expected to change radically year on year, they are not necessarily permanent. Also, explicit attention to strategic efforts to reduce repeats is quite recent, and it may be desirable that attention to it is pushed up the agenda through a KPI.

Third, much that would need to be done to reduce the risk of repeat victimisation locally does not lie under the direct control of the police. Local authorities, voluntary groups such as Neighbourhood Watch and Victim Support, victims themselves, local chambers of commerce, individual businesses and Business Watch, local crime prevention partnerships, and so on may have much more scope actually to implement measures designed to reduce repeats. The police have information on victims, they have expertise, and they can advise/cajole. What they can do directly is limited, though far from negligible (see Annex A). The point here is that police success does lie in part in well targeted cajoling. It is this that a repeat victimisation PI might tap.

6. Crime prevention PIs within forces

In this section some possibilities for crime prevention PIs within forces are mooted. In determining their choice it will be important to be clear what functions the PIs are intended to serve, and to try to anticipate any unwanted unintended side-effect of the sort noted in section 2. It will clearly be sensible to harmonise some intra force PIs with the national crime prevention KPI. Equally, given the danger that work towards achievement of a single priority end risks neglect of other important police crime prevention issues, local PIs will need also to focus on other aspects of performance to put the KPI in context.

Given local differences in problems and opportunities and given the desirability in crime prevention for imaginative initiatives, in-force PIs will need in part to be tailored to locally determined aims. A wide variety of data, collected in differing ways including those discussed in section 3, may be useful. There is scope also for local experimentation in the development and piloting of innovative PIs which might then be adopted or adapted elsewhere. If, for example, robust and inexpensive cost-benefit formulae can be developed to yield workable PIs they could be very useful, and force research departments are well placed to work at these.

There is also scope for making use of repeat victimisation PIs, along the general lines discussed above, for in-force PIs as well as for a national KPI. If the necessary recording and analysis arrangements for a KPI were put in place, much stronger police data for the measurement of needs for special interventions and of the effectiveness of particular initiatives would become available. Those data would, however, often need to be complemented with further information collected either from other sources or directly from intended beneficiaries. These will clearly need to be tailored to particular initiatives, and may include PIs and data sources which were considered less appropriate for a national KPI.

Good practice requires that special crime prevention initiatives be carefully tailored to local conditions, that their effectiveness is ascertained by measurements directly related to intended outcomes, and that lessons learned about what seems to work in what circumstances is disseminated locally.

One possible PI for forces might be the proportion of crime prevention initiatives whose effectiveness is assessed and reported, using locally formulated and agreed PIs tailored to expected crime prevention related outcomes.

Given the importance attached generally to partnership and the particular interest expressed in PIs for crime prevention officers, there follows some brief discussion of possibilities for each of these.

Partnership work

Since much crime prevention work is, perforce, undertaken in partnership, and partnerships require police resources, one measure of performance within forces might usefully assess whether partnerships are operating where needed, and whether they are having their intended crime preventive effects.

A major difficulty in devising a partnership PI is the diversity of partnerships in which the police are involved. Two major types may be discerned through the variety in which the police play a part - those working directly with the public in small sub-beat sized areas and those involving other agencies in more strategic work. Neighbourhood Watch is the commonest example of the first, and Safer Cities Steering Committees would be an example of the second. There are also some groups fitting in between - multi-agency groups involving the public. It has not been found possible to develop a single PI adequate to deal with all forms of partnership. Strategic partnerships probably need to develop their own PIs, and they could usefully focus on repeat victimisation, as discussed above. If they were to do so then accomplishing success in relation to a police repeat victimisation KPI will be so much the easier.

The discussion which follows focuses on police-community partnerships, where the police are the key agency players at sub-beat level. We consider first a PI to measure to what extent police-community partnerships are operating in higher crime neighbourhoods. The following operational definition of a working partnership has been widely accepted as reasonable amongst those spoken to during this work:

A crime prevention partnership may be deemed to exist if a quorate group meets at least four times a year, and if the police are involved by providing information on local crime patterns and advice on what could be done to reduce crime risks.

The population covered by a partnership could refer to individuals, households or addresses. There is some advantage in using addresses, since this would include the non-domestic as well as the domestic potential coverage. The Post-code Address File could provide a count of addresses (see note 4).

It is necessary to define who is covered in police-community partnerships. Are those living within a geographical area included even if they play no active part? Moreover, if an active part is required, how active should it be? Given the changing rates of participation by community members in partnerships, and the difficulties of finding out about it, total numbers in the area covered by the partnership would appear to be preferable.

It might be expected that strategic partnerships will cover the majority of those in each force area. Partnerships with the public will have a lower level of coverage. They are also potentially costly to service, and in some areas very difficult to set up. Comprehensive coverage, whilst a possibility for strategic partnerships, might well not be practicable for active partnerships with the public. The issue is then one of distributing effort to those areas where needs are greatest. The most straightforward measure of need is crime rate, and a PI has been devised to measure coverage of police-public partnerships weighted according to relative crime risk within the force area. Annex C shows the method of calculation.

Tables 3 and 4 give worked examples, assuming very small forces. Each shows a nominal force community partnership coverage of 20%. The effect of weighting in proportion to beat crime rates is that Force Alpha ends up with a score of 24% and Force Beta with a score of 16%. In Force Alpha community partnerships tend to greater concentration in higher crime beats, whereas in Force Beta they tend towards lower crime beats.

Table 3: Example of community partnership PI scores, calculated according to the suggested formula, in Force Alpha					
	Population	Total crimes	Number covered by schemes	Unweighted force coverage	Weighted force coverage
Beat A	10000	1000	2000	5%	4%
Beat B	6000	1000	1500	3.75%	5%
Beat C	8000	800	1000	2.5%	2%
Beat D	12000	1200	1500	3.75%	3%
Beat E	4000	1000	2000	5%	10%
TOTAL	40000	5000	8000	20%	24%

Table 4: Example of community partnership PI scores, calculated according to the suggested formula, in Force Beta					
	Population	Total crimes	Number covered by schemes	Unweighted force coverage	Weighted force coverage
Beat A	5000	1000	500	2.5%	5%
Beat B	8000	400	2500	12.5%	6.25%
Beat C	2000	200	400	2%	2%
Beat D	5000	400	600	3%	2.4%
TOTAL	20000	2000	4000	20%	15.65%

Having established a PI which measures the distribution of partnerships according to need, the next stage is to devise one to measure the relative effectiveness of these partnerships. This might be achieved by examining the degree to which they are able to minimise the mismatch between expected and observed rates of repeat victimisation in relation to those crimes over which it is hoped that police-community partnership can have an impact. This would then feed into a national repeat victimisation KPI. It would also help police management identify where there has been successful practice, which could be disseminated, and also where practice has been less successful and hence additional effort may be needed.

Crime prevention officers

It is difficult to see how general performance indicators could be devised for all Crime Prevention Officers. What is needed will depend on local conditions. It might be hoped that if national objectives are accepted and if the role of CPOs conforms to advice given in the circular of 13th November 1992, local performance indicators attuned to local aims and objectives formulated accordingly will become easier to devise. So far as particular activities and initiatives are concerned, the advice given in Berry and Carter (1992) should be useful.

Some interesting innovations in PI development for the work of CPOs was encountered during the preparation of this report. This involved efforts to remain in touch with the initiatives being developed by CPOs and efforts to help them ascertain their success. In one force area a Crime Prevention Inspector from headquarters regularly visits all divisional CPOs. This allows the centre to remain informed about the work being undertaken. An effort is being made to develop local PIs 'bottom-up'. That is, local CPOs are asked to think through what would count as indicators of success for initiatives they are planning. In this way not only can indicators be used which are sensitive to the particular work being undertaken, but their meaning can be 'owned' by the CPOs. Over a period of time it is hoped that these can then be combined into a higher level indicator to capture force performance. Since the force aims spring in part from the divisions and since crime prevention work is attuned to divisional priorities, it is expected that the locally derived indicators will be relevant to the accomplishment of force objectives as these relate to crime prevention. Moreover, by putting in place arrangements to collect relevant data where outcomes seem to indicate success, this can be broadcast within the force, disseminating ideas about good practice and encouraging further innovation. The travelling inspector, of course, not only finds out what is being done in a division on his visits, but passes on information about what other crime prevention officers are doing. He also becomes a repository of ideas about local PI possibilities.

7. Conclusions

1. Picking PI's is fraught with difficulties. It is essential to be clear about their purpose, and to attend to their potential unintended consequences as well as their intended ones.

2. A series of special problems facing the development of crime prevention performance indicators have dogged efforts for at least a decade.

3. Perfect PIs, especially for crime prevention, will not be found. It will always be possible (easily) to find faults. Selection will have to be based on maximising benefits and minimising costs.

4. The presence of a crime prevention national objective, and corresponding PI, is widely welcomed in stressing the importance of a crucial but under-recognised aspect of policing.

5. The currently most plausible basis for a KPI to meet the needs of the third national, crime prevention objective for policing is changing rates of repeat victimisation, though this will need to be complemented with measures of changes in prevalence.

6. Before a repeat victimisation PI could be implemented fully, alterations in the way incidents are recorded by the police will be needed, to allow victims to be uniquely identified and to allow analysis of patterns of repeats to be computed automatically. This will have to be a first stage objective. Preparing, implementing and benefitting from the results of a repeat victimisation PI could not be accomplished in less than 2-3 years.

7. To respond to the national objective emphasis on local determination of crimes to target for preventative work, it will be necessary to allow choices to be made at Basic Command Unit level. These can then be indexed and aggregated to give a force performance score, though the local figures will be most meaningful to the local publics being served.

8. A benefit of a long term crime prevention PI is that specific crime targets can be changed where necessary, thus avoiding distortive overemphasis on particular crime categories, which might otherwise result.

9. In-force crime prevention PIs will need to be tailored to particular aims and particular schemes. These will best be determined in conjunction with crime prevention officers.

10. A range of approaches to local PIs will be appropriate, using diverse methods of data collection many of which were found not to be so appropriate or practicable for a national KPI. Reformed record keeping, however, will increase the scope for

informative local PIs. It is likely that prevalence and patterns of repeat victimisation will be a useful indicator locally as well as nationally.

11. The meaning of indicators will always need careful interpretation both locally within forces and nationally. Force research departments have a key role in the former case and HMIC in the latter. PIs never speak for themselves.

ANNEX A

Best practice in the delivery of effective crime prevention in the police

In a frequently quoted passage from 1829 Rowan & Mayne, the first Metropolitan Police Commissioners, defined the core function of the police in the following terms:

> 'The principal object to be attained is the prevention of crime. To this end every effort of the police is to be directed.'

Despite this, crime prevention has remained a Cinderella specialism (Harvey et al 1989). There have, though, been various moves in the past three years to alter the image of crime prevention and its relationship to other aspects of operational police work. These can be found in the ACPO paper entitled *The Role of the Crime Prevention Officer* (1991), in the Home Office Circular of 13 November 1992, in Johnson et al (1993), and in the Audit Commission Report, *Helping with Enquiries: Tackling Crime Effectively* (1993). In their separate ways these point towards raising the profile of crime prevention, partnership with the public, integration of prevention with other aspects of police work, and a more strategic approach to the issue. The issue of repeat victimisation is also stressed. It has been found across a range of crime categories that compared to those who have not been a victim of crime those that have are statistically at a higher risk (Farrell & Pease, 1993). The police have an opportunity directly to address this risk through targeted efforts to reduce risks to those against whom reported crimes have been committed.

Figure 1 attempts to distil and structure what appears to be common to the way these documents see crime prevention and police work. This way of construing police crime prevention has been widely accepted amongst those consulted during the preparation of this report.

It can be seen that all crimes are responded to in terms both of detection and prevention. There is complementary work at the level of the incident, the case, the strategic response to emerging crime patterns, and community capacity building for partnerships to fight crime through mobilising capacity for prevention and detection.

The operation of this way of managing police responses to crime depends on integrating detection and prevention, and on giving institutional priority to neither at the expense of the other. It requires a high grade generalist first response from police officers capable of appropriate professional decision-making about arrest and initial crime prevention advice. It also requires capacity to elicit appropriate information to feed into decisions about whether further crime prevention advice by the Home Beat Officer or Crime Prevention Officer is needed and about whether further direct efforts at case detection are worthwhile.

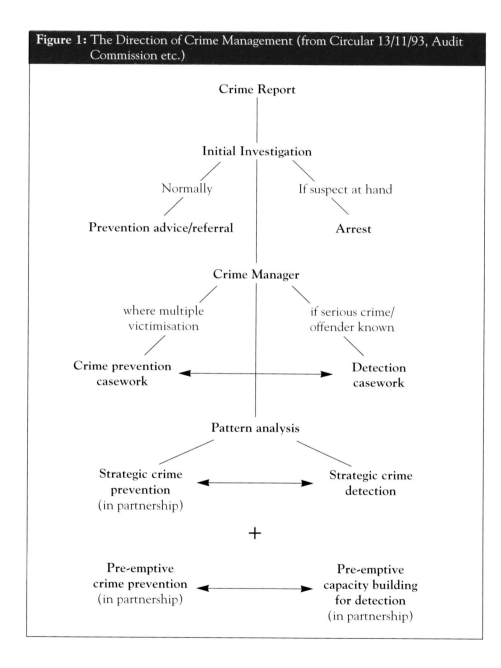

Figure 1: The Direction of Crime Management (from Circular 13/11/93, Audit Commission etc.)

Crime Report

Initial Investigation

Normally — Prevention advice/referral

If suspect at hand — Arrest

Crime Manager

where multiple victimisation — Crime prevention casework

if serious crime/ offender known — Detection casework

Pattern analysis

Strategic crime prevention (in partnership) ↔ Strategic crime detection

+

Pre-emptive crime prevention (in partnership) ↔ Pre-emptive capacity building for detection (in partnership)

In addition this way of managing crime assumes both the computing power and the necessary analytical skills for the information to be processed to feed into strategic responses to crime. By this is meant first, analyses of local crime problems and the orchestration of appropriate preventive initiatives tailored to them, and second, analyses for series of offenses in the service of detection.

The need for specific responsive initiatives will be reduced by pre-emptive crime prevention, for example through advice on design at the planning stage. The capacity for detection will be built, for example through well-delivered community policing. Both of these rely on the formation of partnerships with the public and with voluntary, private and statutory agencies.

This form of response to crime may be accomplished in various administrative arrangements. It may not be easily sustainable, however, unless those involved in organising crime management are versed in crime prevention as well as crime detection. If the senior officer is always a detective or attaches prior importance to detection, prevention is liable to take second place, and the basic (crime prevention) function of policing lost or construed in unduly narrow terms.

If the emerging vision of the location of police crime prevention alongside other operational policing described here is accepted then PIs need to be devised which encourage developments in this direction.

The continuing emphasis on partnership recognises that the police need to work alongside others in statutory, private and voluntary organisations, as well as the public, if they are successfully to put in place many crime preventive measures. Figure 1 indicates, in particular, those points at which partnership with other agencies is clearly needed.

ANNEX B

Method of measuring expected patterns of revictimisation

The basis for the method used to calculate expected patterns of revictimisation is drawn from Trickett et al (1992).

Incidence (I) is defined as the ratio of all crimes (ΣC) to all potential victims (N). Prevalence (P) is defined as the ratio of all actual victims (ΣV) to all potential victims. Concentration (V) is defined as the ratio of all crimes to all actual victims.

Thus, $I = \Sigma C/N$; $P = \Sigma V/N$; and $V = \Sigma C/\Sigma V$.

If each potential victim is equally likely to be selected as an actual victim, for each crime the probability of any particular potential victim actually being victimised is $1/N$. If, also, selection is independent for each crime then the probability that a crime is not committed against any one potential victim is

$$\Pr\{V=0\} = \left(1 - \frac{1}{N}\right)^{\Sigma C} = \left(\frac{N-1}{N}\right)^{\Sigma C}.$$

Therefore, the probability of being a victim is

$$\Pr\{V=1\} = \left[1 - \left(\frac{N-1}{N}\right)^{\Sigma C}\right].$$

The expected number of victims - $E(\Sigma V)$ - from a given population is, thus,

$\Pr\{V=1\} * N$.

Expected concentration is, therefore, $\Sigma C/E(\Sigma V)$.

The expected number of repeats is calculated by subtracting expected number of victims from total crimes, that is,

$\Sigma C - E(\Sigma V)$

The expected number of first repeats uses the same method as that used to calculate prevalence. The potential victim population comprises the number expected to be victimised on the basis of the total number of original crimes. The expected number of those who experience a repeat can then be calculated, using the above formula. This process can then be continued until all crimes are exhausted. The outcome of these calculations is given in Table 1.

Where observed repeat victimisation data are compared with expected patterns, appropriate statistical significance tests can of course be used.

ANNEX C

Method of calculating coverage of police/public partnerships weighted according to relative crime rates

Presently the most detailed level at which crime data are ordinarily available is the beat. A weighting can be determined for each beat through the ratio of the beat crime rate to the force crime rate. For each beat the rate of participation in working partnerships can also be calculated.

The following shows the method used to calculate the weighted coverage of each beat:

$$\left(\frac{BI}{BP}\right)\left(\frac{BCR}{CCR}\right)\left(\frac{BP}{CP}\right)$$

BI refers to beat involvement, the number in the beat covered by a partnership; BP is the number of potential beat participants, BCR is the overall beat crime rate (number of beat crimes divided by beat population); CCR is the corresponding constabulary crime rate (number of constabulary crimes divided by constabulary population); and CP is the constabulary population of potential partnership participants. BI/BP measures the rate of participation within the beat; BP/CP measures the size of the beat relative to the constabulary as a whole; and BCR/CCR controls for the relative extent of the crime problem in each beat. The sum of the scores for each beat in a Force multiplied by 100 would give the percentage of risk covered by partnership. (The calculation for each beat simplifies to BI/BP X BC/CC, where BC refers to beat crime and CC to constabulary crime.)

The intention of the calculation sketched above is to control for the relative seriousness of the crime problem in different areas in assessing the extent of partnership, rather than measuring it simply in relation to the total population of potential members. This has been done to emphasise the greater potential for creating real crime prevention in partnerships where crime rates are higher.

References

ACPO (1991) 'The Role of the Crime Prevention Officer'

Audit Commission (1993) *Helping with Enquiries: Tackling Crime Effectively*, London: HMSO.

Berry, G. & M. Carter (1992) *Assessing Crime Prevention Initiatives: The First Steps*, Crime Prevention Unit Paper 31, London: Home Office.

Bridgeman, C. & A. Sampson (1994) *Wise After the Event: Tackling Repeat Victimisation*. A Report by the National Board for Crime Prevention, London: Home Office.

Ekblom, P. (1989) 'Evaluation: The Management of Uncertainty', in C. Kemp (ed) *Current Issues in Criminological Research*, Bristol: Bristol Centre for Criminal Justice.

Ekblom, P. & K. Pease (Forthcoming) 'Evaluating Crime Prevention', in *Crime & Justice*, Vol. 19.

Farrell, G. & A. Buckley (1993) 'Repeat victimisation as a police performance indicator: a case study of a domestic violence unit in Merseyside', presented at the British Criminology Conference, University of Wales, Cardiff.

Farrell, G. & K. Pease (1993) *Once Bitten, Twice Bitten: Repeat Victimisation and its implications for Crime Prevention*, Crime Prevention Unit Paper 46, London: Home Office.

Harvey, L., Grimshaw, P. & K. Pease (1989) 'Crime prevention delivery: the work of Crime Prevention Officers', in R. Morgan & D. Smith (eds) *Coming to Terms with Policing*, London: Routledge, pp. 82-96.

Home Office (1992) *Development of Crime Prevention Work*, un-numbered Circular of 13th November.

Home Office (1993) *Circular No 17/1993: Performance indicators for the police*.

Home Office (1993) *Police Reform White Paper: A Police Service for the Twenty-First Century - The Government's Proposals for the Police Service in England and Wales*, London: HMSO.

Husain, S. (1988) *Neighbourhood Watch in England and Wales: A Locational Analysis*, Crime Prevention Unit Paper 47, London: Home Office.

Johnson, V., Shapland, J. & P. Wiles (1993) *Developing Police Crime Prevention Management and Organisational Change*, Crime Prevention Unit Paper 41, London: Home Office.

Laycock, G. (1989) *An Evaluation of Domestic Security Surveys*, Crime Prevention Unit Paper 18, London: Home Office.

Mayhew, P., Elliott, D. & L. Dowds (1989) *The 1988 British Crime Survey*, Home Office Research Study 111, London: HMSO.

Morris, P. & K. Heal (1981) *Crime Control and the Police: A Review of the Research*, Home Office Research Study 67, London: HMSO.

Pawson, R. & N. Tilley (1994) 'What works in evaluation research?', *British Journal of Criminology*, Vol 34, No. 1, pp. 291-306.

Smith, P. (Forthcoming) 'On the unintended consequences of publishing performance data in the public sector', *International Journal of Public Administration*.

Trickett, A., Osborn, D., Seymour, J. & K. Pease (1992) 'What is different about high crime areas?', *British Journal of Criminology*, Vol 32, No 1, pp. 81-89.

CRIME PREVENTION UNIT SERIES PAPERS

1. **Reducing Burglary: a study of chemists' shops.** Gloria Laycock. 1985.

2. **Reducing Crime: developing the role of crime prevention panels.** Lorna J. F. Smith and Gloria Laycock. 1985.

3. **Property Marking: a deterrent to domestic burglary?** Gloria Laycock. 1985.

4. **Designing for Car Security: towards a crime free car.** Dean Southall and Paul Ekblom. 1986.

5. **The Prevention of Shop Theft: an approach through crime analysis.** Paul Ekblom. 1986.

6. **Prepayment Coin Meters: a target for burglary.** Nigel Hill. 1986.

7. **Crime in Hospitals: diagnosis and prevention.** Lorna J. F. Smith.

8. **Preventing Juvenile Crime: the Staffordshire Experience.** Kevin Heal and Gloria Laycock. 1987.

9. **Preventing Robberies at Sub-Post Offices: an evaluation of a security initiative.** Paul Ekblom. 1987.

10. **Getting the Best out of Crime Analysis.** Paul Ekblom. 1988.

11. **Retail Crime: Prevention through Crime Analysis.** John Burrows. 1988.

12. **Neighbourhood Watch in England and Wales: a locational analysis.** Sohail Husain. 1988.

13. **The Kirkholt Burglary Prevention Project, Rochdale.** David Forrester, Mike Chatterton and Ken Pease with the assistance of Robin Brown. 1988.

14. **The Prevention of Robbery at Building Society Branches.** Claire Austin. 1988.

15. **Crime Prevention and Racial Harassment in Asian-run Small Shops: the scope for prevention.** Paul Ekblom and Frances Simon with the assistance of Sneh Birdi. 1988.

16. **Crime and Nuisance in the Shopping Centre: a case study in crime prevention.** Susan Phillips and Raymond Cochrane. 1988.

17. **The Prevention of Fraud.** Michael Levi. 1988.

18. **An Evaluation of Domestic Security Surveys.** Gloria Laycock. 1989.

19. **Downtown Drinkers: the perceptions and fears of the public in a city centre.** Malcolm Ramsey. 1989.

20. **The Management and Prevention of Juvenile Crime Problems.** Barrymore Cooper. 1989.

21. **Victim Support and Crime Prevention in an Inner-City Setting.** Alice Sampson and Graham Farrell. 1990.

22. **Lagerland Lost? An experiment in keeping Drinkers off the street in central Coventry and elsewhere.** Malcolm Ramsey. 1990.

23. **The Kirkholt Burglary Prevention Project: Phase II.** David Forrester, Samantha Frenz, Martin O'Connell and Ken Pease. 1990.

24. **Probation Practice in Crime Prevention.** Jane Geraghty. 1991.

25. **Lessons from a Victim Support Crime Prevention Project.** Alice Sampson. 1991.

26. **The Prevention of Cheque and Credit Card Fraud.** Michael Levi, Paul Bissell and Tony Richardson. 1991.

27. **Making Crime Prevention Pay: initiatives from business.** John Burrows. 1991.

28. **The Influence of Street Lighting on Crime and Fear of Crime.** Stephen Atkins, Sohail Husain and Angele Storey. 1991.

29. **The Effect of Better Street Lighting on Crime and Fear: a Review.** Malcolm Ramsay with the assistance of Rosemary Newton. 1991.

30. **Reducing Crime on the London Underground.** Barry Webb and Gloria Laycock. 1992.

31. **Assessing Crime Prevention Initiatives: The First Steps.** Geoff Berry and Mike Carter. 1992.

32. **Tackling Car Crime.** Barry Webb and Gloria Laycock. 1992.

33. **Car Theft in England and Wales: The Home Office Car Theft Index.** George Houghton. 1992.

34. **Preventing Car Crime in Car Parks.** Barry Webb, Ben Brown and Katherine Bennett. 1992.

35. **Closed Circuit Television in Public Places.** Terry Honess and Elizabeth Charman. 1992.

52. **Inter-Agency Crime Prevention: Organising Local Delivery.** Mark Liddle and Loraine Gelsthorpe. 1994.

53. **Crime Prevention and Inter-Agency Cooperation.** Mark Liddle and Loraine Gelsthorpe. 1994

   Inter-Agency Crime Prevention: Further Issues *(Supplementary Paper to Crime Prevention Unit Papers 52 & 53).*

54. **Crime on Industrial Estates.** Valerie Johnston, Maria Leitner, Joanna Shapland & Paul Wiles. 1994.

CRIME DETECTION AND PREVENTION SERIES

55. **Witness Intimidation: Strategies for Prevention.** Warwick Maynard. 1994.

56. **Preventing Vandalism: What Works?** Mary Barker, Cressida Bridgeman. 1994.